"Patrycja Humienik picks up where the great Polish poets of the twentieth century left off, writing of exile, war, fragmented families, and grief for a ruined environment. And yet, her mind is utterly contemporary and new, searching and witty, always striving towards a politics of solidarity with the Other—the reader, the ancestors, the daughters of immigrants. The poet's wondrous imagination flows like water across these pages, picking up the peculiar and astonishing facts of life on earth, like 'kiwis ripening in early December,' a sky like a cicatrix, 'the presence / of screens' that shape memory, or 'eyelashes beating / against time.' *We Contain Landscapes* introduces a gorgeous, determined, and vibrant new voice to American poetry, a voice that dances with, exults in, and blurs the boundaries of the lyric."

—ARIA ABER,
author of *Good Girl*

"In Patrycja Humienik's book, *We Contain Landscapes*, there is strangeness around every corner—the speaker 'argue[s] like a window,' a 'head [is] full of fragments,' or 'the digital / leaves teeth marks on my thinking.' Here are intensely beautiful poems that arrange perception and then rearrange it, in the way that identity and memory do."

—VICTORIA CHANG,
author of *With My Back to the World*

"In *We Contain Landscapes*, Patrycja Humienik illuminates the sticky insides of longing and the crisis of returning to ourselves in the process of returning home. This collection speaks to the heart of the immigrant daughter, and the daughter responds: 'yes, I speak to you / in sweat.'"

—CAMONGHNE FELIX,
author of *Dyscalculia:*
A Love Story of Epic Miscalculations

"Daughter of immigrants, Patrycja Humienik confronts the agonizing betrayals of nation-states, as well as the pressures of sexuality, the obliterating lure of the internet. She writes with a physicality that is utterly mesmerizing. Shot through with radiance and self-possession, Humienik's poems are reminders that life at the edge of exorbitant longing can feel more free, more alive."

—JOANNA KLINK,
author of *The Nightfields*

We Contain Landscapes

We Contain Landscapes

Patrycja Humienik

POEMS

TIN HOUSE / PORTLAND, OREGON

First US Edition 2025
Printed in the United States of America

Manufacturing by Kingery Printing Company
Interior design by Beth Steidle

Library of Congress Cataloging-in-Publication Data

Names: Humienik, Patrycja, author.
Title: We contain landscapes : poems / Patrycja Humienik.
Description: First US edition. | Portland, Oregon : Tin House, 2025.
Identifiers: LCCN 2024051377 | ISBN 9781963108040 (paperback) |
ISBN 9781963108101 (ebook)
Subjects: LCGFT: Poetry.
Classification: LCC PS3608.U448 W4 2025 | DDC 811/.6—dc23/eng/20241108
LC record available at https://lccn.loc.gov/2024051377

Tin House
2617 NW Thurman Street, Portland, OR 97210
www.tinhouse.com

DISTRIBUTED BY W. W. NORTON & COMPANY

1 2 3 4 5 6 7 8 9 0

for my beloveds

Have you known
known in every pore of your skin
how your eyes your hands your sex your soft heart
must be thrown away
must be wept away
must be invented all over again

—JULIO CORTÁZAR

TRANS. STEPHEN KESSLER

Każdy przecież początek
to tylko ciąg dalszy

—WISŁAWA SZYMBORSKA

Contents

•

•

•

We Contain Landscapes

An Anchor Is an Argument

Growing up, I despised the metronome,
    its insistence on orderly time, the lie.

Counting the seconds between flash & stampede
    in my childhood bed—storms full of horses.

A woman in the night must be sensitive to sound
    in case the sound has a motive.

Anchor is an argument.
    A child is the wrong technology for dreaming.

I play Comptine d'un autre été
    whenever I come across a piano.

I play with feeling,
    but I can never remember the ending.

Eros and Sorrow

lance every boat anchored in memory's
harbor. Offshore, someone is moaning
in swells that unswell. Cacophony
of bells. Bowl of honey pelvis
rocked to pleasure, rocked to tears.

I'm crying after sex. Kettle's going off
and off—the arrows in that
sound could puncture even steel.
I pour slowly, opening a curtain
in the back of mind.

Out the window, the diving swallows
thieve my periphery
with ceaseless flight;
        I came from this theft
of what cannot be mine. Not time

or rivers. Even my devotions
refuse possession.
Tiny, entangled butterflies chart
a constellation around my head,
circumventing the lens.

The oak on the bluff has a hole in it
like an exposed heart I want to make
myself small enough to climb into.
But trees don't need hearts.
I'm carving a face into the stump

in my sternum before it splinters
to kindling. I'm harvesting
nettles from forests half-sunk
in my ribs. Marsh in mouth,
a hurricane wept into 29 tabs open.

I'd draw you a map if it would not divide.

We contain landscapes.
They do not belong to us.

Failed Essay on Repressed Sexuality

The internet was my childhood refuge.
It's where I practice still. Erase
my browsing history.

At the strip club, a friend leans over to say
the search for a moral politic is a failure.
How it mirrors a religious pursuit, that fervor.

I agree, then disagree. I'm watching my favorite dancer,
feeling the ghost of my teenage body.
A river rushing superimposed boundaries.

Do to me what sunlight does to a river.

No Common Language

Mama says people play gods

Not every family has a common language

Current sleeps in still water

If I argue like a window

Sculpt the immaterial subject

Verdigris around the eyes

Glass bottles fill with tears

The pond widens as days shorten

Words form little charging bulls

The woods quiet except for their pulse

America,

I keep only the finest of a thousand lies

Salt of the Earth

In a blurry photo from my first trip to Poland at 19, me and my godmother, one of my mother's ten siblings, are laughing together, a thousand feet into the earth, in a 13th century chapel made entirely of salt. Sculptures carved of rock salt, rock salt chandeliers, a rock salt Last Supper.

> In childhood, she was one of many names.
> A voice on the phone. A formal exchange.

Table salt was made there from the upwelling brine. Upwelling the closest thing resembling a wall in water.

.

> I feared the door. Someone coming to take
> my parents away.
>
> *Illegals— Taking*
> *American jobs—*
>
> In classroom debates about immigration,
> I kept quiet.

.

Watching my godmother watch her grandchildren running the edges of the creek I wanted to call a river. Slicing bugs from mushrooms picked before dawn. Dropping the slivers quick into buckets. Asking when will I have children, and haven't I had enough school already, and how is it that we have so much debt in America?

.

Shielded by whiteness,
assumed to be documented.

Threaten the economy— One out of every 12 newborns—

•

In another aunt's kitchen, over rosehip tea, she said I wasn't as spoiled as they'd expected, for an amerykanka. I was proud, and devastated to be called American.

•

Providing an advantage to family members seeking to secure citizenship—

Silence both protected and betrayed.

•

At 22, running up a blur of pines, beyond my uncle's turkeys and geese, to where my mama grew up picking blueberries, I planted a little tree. Where I'm invited to return.

•

The difference between a river and a creek is that
from a creek, no new branches are formed.

Anchor baby, n. Offensive

On Self-Deceit

I tie myself to the good-girl mast
but it's a punctured raft on land.
Golden grass stains both my knees.
I say *sorry*. I say *thank you*.
I say *please*.

      I wait for someone to untie the knots.
      It's not a question of show or tell.
      It's not a question.

If I set fire to the image. Fire clears the land
of excess. But the mind remains
unleveled.

The forest knows

  there are needed fires,
and fires birthed by selfishness.

      In *Self-Deceit #1*, Francesca Woodman, naked
      on all fours, curves her torso around a desolate corner,
      toward a square mirror against the wall.
      Looking down. Averting her own gaze.

Some eruptions start small in us.
I like to think I could feel the blood quicken.

Rage seems ordinary, easy enough.
But it takes something from you
to travel there.

The volcano I live near could take me
out, make ash the last word.

Parts of me are dying.

I don't have to walk the cemeteries
to speak to them.

To hide or seek might look the same.

What I'm looking for
is subvocal.

Saint Hyacinth Basilica

House of yelling, scent of hyacinth.
Back then my head was full of fragments.
Of a question I buried and unburied
in the dirt. Flower brain unblinking.

Drenched in gossamer. Webs glint then
disappear. Subject fatigued by a silken un-
ribboning. Undoing takes more effort than
you'd think. Here, the subject was supposed to
be a child. Able to take a joke.

What makes a child serious could be called
devotion. It is beyond obedience.
Kneeling in recognition of one's smallness
in the vast. I learned about love that way. But
when devotion is self-betrayal, what then?

•

When devotion is self-betrayal,
the body knows. The first time I fainted,
I was a choirgirl. Someone caught me just
before I hit my head. Damn pillar. The saints &

clergy in the dome's 3,000-square-foot
mural looking down on me. Our Lady
of Częstochowa crowned in ten pounds of gold.
Jackowo, center of Polonia. Three
steeples visible from the Kennedy

Expressway. Glazed terracotta, brick & stone.
Three pairs of heavy bronze doors I never
touched. Girl or woman, holy only
what's done to me. I don't agree. Still, that
story leaves a mark. I rarely touch myself.

•

I rarely touch myself—the story leaves a mark.
The sword struck twice Our Lady's face at Jasna
Góra, where the horses refused to go on.
Like millions, I kneeled at her shrine. One

uncle took me there en route to Warszawa,
fasting like his grandmother. Twice a week. If there
were photographs of her, they burned. My great-
grandmother hated artificial light. This
stubbornness enough to imagine we were

alike. Did she steal pleasure in the pasture
like her daughter's daughter? My mother, swinging
onto cows' backs with her brothers. Two decades
later, reunited, cheeks streaked with charcoal.
For a moment terribly close to childhood.

•

Each moment risks proximity to childhood.
Splayed out on the rocks, near the sprawl of lake,
that inland sea. It was spring, I think. We were
supposed to be in school. Driving for the sake

of going somewhere. Later, standing
at my friend's kitchen sink—I don't know
how long I stayed there, observing a tiny
jade on the windowsill, ache of the
weight of living in each oval leaf,

luminous though it was, easily engulfed—
I sensed, intensely, an older version of my
self. These selves. Embracing now. & Time,
beating heart, draping its diaphanous wings over
all of us, saying *here we are here we are.*

.

Here we are, here we are, all of us
singing. Such was my dream of faith. Silver
hymn to slip on. No thirst. A river alongside
the whole way. I went to the desert instead,

praying for the pearl beyond the din of text
like a square jaw, clenched fist, asking to be
spared from analysis. To be abandoned
by dreaming. A woman acted upon.
But I move otherwise. That a daughter

carries the desire of many mothers before
is a hunch I visit in my sleep. Faces
forming a mass of land. Longitude. I long to
plant flowers there. Dry them upside down. Quiet
the house of yelling, stench of hyacinth.

Figuration

My lover with the cello between his knees, bow hovering

There's a place we go when we talk about empire

It is not abstraction

When I try to help my father prepare for the citizenship test he says, *That's not
    one of the questions*

Gas nearing $7 a gallon

My mother doesn't miss a day of work

Leftovers wedged in the widened space between my gums and the fake tooth

My father calls me his American dream

A good daughter is a secret keeper

I suppose I am to live like a kind of evidence

Sorry for Taking

so long to call back
the first time the phone
rang I was beneath a
bridge when you rang
again the roar of cars and
cargo overhead made it too
loud to hear you sense of
sea partially obscured
by traffic but felt
when the phone rang
a third time I thought I
could be beneath
you could be water
on the other line if your
voice weren't so ironed-on
when I answer I don't ask
if you still iron your shirts
every morning I let you
talk coral tone once
hot pink got too hot
bleached further down
darkness giving shelter
to shells mouthing
open and *close* when
I hang up I'm sweating I
feel the plastic floating
toward everything

Recurring

Whatever the time of day, whether the sky is florescent,
    or fluorescent, or dissolving color

to impression, or I'm not tracking the sky, perhaps for once
    not inhabiting the subjunctive mood,

whether with a beloved, whose face is turning away—no
    matter if I am in fact alone, on a beach,

looking out toward the doctrine of horizon, there is
    always, in the dream, a wall of water

before me, impossible to outrun, azure, cruel, how
    beauty exists with no regard for goodness or the living,

and if I'm inside, even if I cannot see that weather,
    I can feel it, eroding the floorboards, disintegrating

reason, ceaseless. It has an appetite.

I Found a Lover and We Left the City

temporarily. Crackle of the fire said as much.
Temple into the sprawl of limbs, which came later.

First the alchemists: oysters we ate quietly as we could,
laughing, not saying a word, eyes full of language.

And it wasn't that no one had ever touched me before,
but it had never been like this. Tunnel-less. Not a search

for a prize, zippered pearl to coax out of grieving.
Not the scarcity of hardship or the dismissal of it, but we did

look up: airglow: sky a cicatrix: purpling, paler. Damage,
and the need to undo it—not to fix, but to unribbon

the past. My mama grew up in a rural place, rolling hills
of jade, my name betrayed her wish to leave that lack.

Szlachetnie urodzona: desire for wealth and its associated ease.
I don't blame her for using a name like a tool for weeding.

I, too, prune and tug at my story, but she wanted me to live
up to my name, and for that I might blame her. I learn other names,

plants that please me: forsythia, hyacinth, pyracantha; my lover
gives me a dried bouquet. I prefer weeping

willow, even seaweed, something of water. I want
not to say this but to be understood with my eyes, the way

I was, for a moment, by the fire. But some lovers are not for lasting, though that part comes later, if I, must I, tell the truth.

Letter to Another Immigrant Daughter

for Itiola

Like my father, I love trains and
beautiful women. When have you let yourself go
off the rails?

I first wrote off-kilter. But *kilter* sounds
like a word that would position me
at an edge. I'd look out and call the view

stunning, slip a hand in my pocket to touch
other borders, feeling for the place
in the linen worn thin from repeated touch, that cliff

of too much, trench of a thought
ached over, aching still.

There are train rides I wish I'd taken.

Clamor on all sides en route to the dining car
watching rivers and the trees at their banks
hinged in splintered urge—

They clench their roots & each other close
so as not to fall in.

Let landscapes
skip rocks across our faces
pressed up against the glass. Tell me a story.
Tell me everything. Your laugh widens the gaze.

       If the trees watch us in one flicker they see
where breath is held.

I'm not sure a daughter can ever be grateful enough.

Some days I am thankless.
       Fogging up the window drawing hearts.

Archival

I descend the gallery stairs
  to the history of women
where my legs are cut off at the knee.

Carved with the knife of ecstasy.
  I lie down halved
next to the instrument of my thinking.

Not the bodiless head
  but feet, their subduction,
in bronze, polymer, gypsum.

Migration is the story of longing
  is the story. To risk
rupture for rapture.

Footprints on the ceiling,
  a ladder I tug down
   from its primeval coil.

Steel, fiberglass, and copper,
  where finish splits from color,
longing is ribless as a scorpion.

Do not fix me to the vanishing
  point. I cannot afford to lose
what I cannot possess.

On Devotion

Not the splendor of the dead kings' baths but the peacocks
    demanding devotion   is it devotion

to pour a glass of water for your lover?

.

Easy to confuse habit with ritual,
      ritual with devotion, devotion with desire

.

Alone in the back of a candlelit mass
in English, not the vaulted frescoes of my childhood basilica,
mumbled prayers in Polish   lit a candle
for my mother's parents who I never met   I had questions
for God   *do you renounce imperialism?*

.

Winters ago on the phone a friend saying, *jealousy is good because it is a
form of protection*, but what if protection is a form of harm?

Winter again   snowed in   my lover shoveling
flake after flake out my mouth and into the slush pile   a pathway out
to where the roads are closed

.

That it rarely snows where I now live delights and disturbs me
	e.g., kiwis ripening in early December

The midwestern Polish priest, a family friend,
sends conspiracy theory videos via WhatsApp

Along the fence strung lights remind me of snow
where white camellias grow instead

.

That I want to see every body of water, lava, lands I don't know the names for,
	the Red Sea—

isn't it enough to have seen flamingos
pink with feeding in the salt flats in the driest desert in the world?

.

Sometimes I think of God while washing my feet
I think of where I have not walked   my longing
to go further

I Defer Pleasure

Let it build. Become
a wall. Then four. I install a spotlight,
prepare my speech, knock over a chair, try
to negotiate geometry. First a house, a block,
then a whole city of wanting. In the city of my almost,
a pianist rolls her upright Wurlitzer uphill,
sits at the apex to play a nocturne
with eyes closed. On the downhill, racks full of fabric
the color of the crest of a wave when the sun hits.
Funyuns at the corner store. Children chalk the sidewalk,
charting territory for hopscotch. Pipelines beneath
boxes 1 through 7. Traffic sign, sinews taut.
A man with palms outstretched.
A man in a blinking box signaling to hurry up and cross,
darting eyes saying, *don't look me so long in the eyes.*
Around the corner, at the flower stand,
I adorn myself. Snatch every tulip, lilac,
hyacinth, night-blooming jasmine, rose—I gather
all blossoms to crown, fill my pockets, stuff
the remaining petals in my mouth. By fistful, by boatload,
I play pretend. That what I won't let myself have
is my horizon. Water that won't run out.
I walk three blocks to reach the edge
of an inland sea, minnows circling my feet.
Now the water is oil. The water is lead.

How American

My father buys blue paint to address the rust.
A bald eagle passes three times on the hunt.
After eighteen months apart, we don't know what to say.

I search for the names of birds. Try to describe
their trills, warbles, screeches to Google. Not faith
in language so much as faith in the effort.

Some days I love the sound of my own voice.
I could be cursed. Worse, scattered to fragments
across the earth like Echo

who, in one version, angers the god
of pastures, refusing to yield to man.
I argue as though I can change my father.

Insist on walking the shoreline alone.
Consider the cargo ship EVERGREEN.
Crack a mineralized shell. Crawl out. Hunted.

Borderwound

Great Polish poets were born in cities that no longer belong to Poland. Now Lithuania, Belarus, Ukraine. My people claim the imagined place. Guarded by the Gate of Dawn, the Cross of Saint Euphrosyne, the golden lion with its coat of arms, the crowned eagle. The idea of nation is a record full of _____. Anzaldúa wrote, *the U.S.-Mexican border es una herida abierta.* Scrawled in black marker on a wall in Bulgaria, EVERY BORDER IS A WOUND. On how many walls, in how many languages is it written? Wounds unlatch on every continent. A map only approximates. Each time Poland was erased, the Wisła river remained. Can a river unwound? There's a Polish saying that quiet waters tear the banks. *Cicha woda* coming for my outlines. On a strip of polluted beach beneath the Poniatowski Bridge, faces warmed by the golden hour, a painter tells me, breathless, that Warszawa was magnificent before the war. The past disrupts the current. It happens all the time. We climb to see the river at dusk, a different scale, tilting: past-future, future-past.

The Pipe Organ

When mass was over
        I'd turn my gaze from the altar

    and look up
    to see where the music came from

Pressurized air sculpts
a resonant pitch

I live not naming what I want
which means I am a coward

      Timbre of the unsaid
      flushing the house with worship

Avoiding great pleasure
to avoid great pain

is a kind of obedience
antithetical to music

Floodplain

It isn't that the flood rids us of memory,
no. It shapes memory, cracks

our knuckles. Across the Atlantic,
my aunts and uncles rise early

for the blessing later.
Anoint tired, thirsty skin with oil

after a day's work. That's elegance to me.
Drought or torrent, someone works

the land. Along the Pacific,
someone picks fruit I know the name of.

Don't you ever wish to stay
in bed for days? Touch

a deluge, eroding structure,
toppling every monument.

Violence held in stone. To try
to contain anything is

to rid it of water. Admit that
the water is rising.

Admit that
you need a flood.

Holding Ground

Waking up and scrolling, into a state. I'm searching for a digital anchor.
It would be simpler if each coordinate corresponded with a single feeling.

•

Near the cemetery, Elisa points out a building with the sign, Life Storage.
Another building marked, Signs.

•

IV full of ink, a spreading heat—I tell myself it's just sensation, try not to clench
my jaw. I'm maneuvered in and out of the machine, listening for automated
instructions to hold my breath, to breathe again.

•

After some internal debate, I put the eye-shaped earrings with a dangling
jewel tear in my virtual shopping cart, use my credit card.

•

The skaters in the parking lot are versed in failure as a practice.

•

Pulled over on a dark, rainy night where the highway becomes a bridge,
the man who rear-ended me says, *Peace be with you*, with a little bow.

Later, he refuses to pay for the damages.
I google him, find out he's a corporate exec.

•

An anchorage location may be chosen for its holding ground.
In poor holding ground, only the weight of an anchor matters.

Some feelings are vaults. Other feelings cling to their origins.

•

It's not weight exactly, but the digital
leaves teeth marks on my thinking. I can feel the presence
of screens in my memory, exerting pressure.

•

On the tarmac, I text Gabby a song, mention the tears streaming down my face,
the plane slowly gaining speed. She texts back, *Listening to the song you sent,*
watching you in your plane taking off in my mind's eye like a movie.

•

I'm obsessed with gerunds, their ongoingness. I try to use them **less**
after a mentor tells me -ings are corrosive.

•

In flight, there's an electric-pink line through suspended clouds, right through their
middle, network of city lights below. The line so perfect it looks photoshopped.
Beauty is exacting.

The night becomes clear enough for a moonbow
I won't likely see. I keep looking.

Because Horse Is the Closest I Can Get to It

Cloud shadows cross snow
Cursory as I imagine us

On horseback through sagebrush
And icy rivers even in the dark

The horse in my mind knows the moon
Well enough to not need to speak to it

When I try to talk to horses I watch their feet
Aware of their weight I try to feel my own

A horse knows when you don't know
Where your own two feet are

Picture us running
So fast my mind could quiet

Wilno

Of the dream I remember only a flash:
my grandfather playing the violin, chin tucked
in music. In life, he never played the instrument.

My father tells me his father, born near Wilno,
spent a month freezing in the wooden wagon
of a freight train, breath forming ice in the hay.

He left his birthplace to keep his country.
There are stories I long for
from their source.

I watch YouTube videos of my Dziadek's favorite
music: Czerwone Gitary, Halina Kunicka. Listen
on loop to Filipinki's rendition of Ave Maria.

Dziadek is around you then.
My father texts me a photo of his father's grave,
Babcia's name on the tomb prepared beside.

One Saturday, I had to stand in front of the class
to recite Mickiewicz's famous lines to Lithuania:
Litwo, Ojczyzno moja! ty jesteś jak zdrowie...

We didn't discuss fathers or
the construct of a nation-state.
How words circulate, thicken

the blood over time. Summoned
like a river by a larger body, I am carried
in sleep toward inherited longings.

Objects

On a bus in Chile, I lose my grandmother's
bursztyn ring, its amber from the Bałtyk shores.

In memory's temporal house
a woman walks her cows out
to where the river meets the sea.

I'm always watching two bodies of water converge.

The river acquires density.
Saltwater lets itself be pressed down.

Wind blows directly into our kissing.
Spares us sand but not air's loneliness.

I ask my lover to lie on top of me
so I can make a lasting imprint.

7,000 miles north I lie awake listening
for the romance and terror of passing trains
along the Pacific,

their crusade of commerce, bridging
distances, relentless lust for
objects.

Damn I miss that oval ring.
I hope someone's granddaughter is wearing it.

Ecotones

Little birds whose names I don't know,
       underbellies a shock of citrus,
swoop & flutter. With an ease I envy.
       Behind my looking is the scene's
competing memory. Ears ringing
       with interrupted
sleep. Scrolling.
       Dissociation is one way to survive.

Twice daily, the estuary is flooded with salt
at high tide. Draining twice a day at low.

O tenderness, I'm walking toward you.
Why are you pulling away?

Letter to Another Immigrant Daughter

for Joyce

Considering the long arc
of lineage, there are questions
our mothers may never answer.
I want to know the details
that crossed seas, stitched
into fabrics she keeps unworn
in a trunk at the foot of her bed.
Who did she want to be when
her childhood home burned down?
When she worked in the tobacco factory?
When she boarded her first plane
to a new life? I study the circumstances
of my arrival. *I build a cathedral*
inside my skull. In a stained-glass window
there's a woman I don't recognize.
Tears in her eyes. But I taste the salt.
There are questions I don't know
how to ask. Omissions form
minerals at the bottom of a well
where coins drop unheard.
I am guilty of writing to be saved.
I am guilty of trying to save.
The water I am made of asks me
to quiet in it.

We

who am i   to speak

                              for anyone   but my

many selves

here: this page: fingers running over: you: yes, you, dear

reader: have we—   do i—   know you?

we? as in all bodies? ever

  touched: in passing: past: i was born
an ocean away from   where i was conceived   circling a prayer:
  longing   bending over, under   how water goes: grief
                                      pooling in my clavicles:

              &   all   who   came before:
is we a home?

                                      who is not
              here: left   out:

                        in Spanish: nosotros: otro:
                                              as in other

      when i learn a language not spoken in my family
                              am i trying to expand the we?

      we is my   in Polish   the y softer
                        not possession: it's not mine

          to belong to: be longed for   is we   a longing

42

Good Friday

The busted rosary encircling my wrist
makes little silver thorns where it split.
It's not fasting I have a problem with,

or even the temporary absence of music.
I would like to fast from screens, lab tests,
diagnoses. From the judgment

I inherited. Economies of lack. Piousness
waged like mercy. But I'm trying
to pay my debts and get

my teeth fixed. Even water has a price.
I was taught it must be sanctified
to be considered holy.

Self-Portrait as Hélène Delmaire's Painting
of a Woman in the Bathtub

whose face you cannot see. Head to knees,
back bare, shoulders sloped toward shadow.
                    I bow to the ache. Surrender in
the color between greens: my thinking
        serpentine: cinching the waist of the world.
The bathwater is still, but the walls
                are moving. When two paths cross, the colors
bleed. Muddied pinks, burst of rivered yellow.
        Winter in the plains. How when spring came,
it was earned. I am listening for
                the echo of a bell beneath my tongue.
The condition of woman is to stay.
The condition of woman is to grieve.
        Weeping, I refuse—

Night

I. *Pluck*

I am belly up beneath the dogwood plucking petals
when Night comes out sprawls out beside me

They say, *if you want a name*
I have a fissure

Night knows I long for a new name
Night's pronouns are they/them

I nod   we toss
    voices in familiar lilt &
      scatter

They say, *you are swooned by seeming ground*
what is beneath that?

Pollen untethers
         one answer
     from another

       shattering into

              Once upon a time
            in an alley, city gave Night their quiet back
            at what cost I do not ask

Night is matter of fact: *no matter*
how much salt
is in your head   *you still have*
a body

II. *Aubade in Which I Linger*

Night slips from my vision grainy
as we make our way up the dirt path.

I let myself be held by sandstone
harboring a prehistoric sea.

Dryness tunnels my nostrils,
could clear every longing from me,

if I were as mutable and eager to be changed
as I say. There are days I beg to be left,

to see what I've been withholding.
Night knows I'm unlikely to leave first.

In florid glow, lulled to an almost-sleep,
the stirring morning sifts me.

III. *Cargo*

Night arrives at the door with a lidded platter of chocolate chip cookies vegan *since you can't have dairy* unlaces their boots and sits across from me responds to my raised how-did-you-find-me-in-the-woods eyebrows *I knew you'd be here trying to clear your head* crossing and uncrossing their limbs hair spiraling up toward the ceiling as they stand to stretch then down on the floor telling me to come press my back against the ground so I do and we stare up where the paint cracks the rafters making a triangle I press my heels into the ground feel my back rollicking into a momentary bridge to let invisible ships pass then lower the arch the lock this fixed chamber trying to lengthen trying to will breath into recurring ache the ships having taken their cargo elsewhere I say *I don't want any more stuff* and Night says *I know* and I'm crying and we've got chocolate in our teeth and when I wake I'm alone again not far from sea

Acid Reflux

Did it make a home inside
your chest? What is the softest thing
you've ever held hostage? At what age
did you first hide your truest
feeling? What feeling then
eclipsed the truer one?
Who did you blame?

Porous

East of the city I find dolomite.
Its crystals wear curved faces
      stretched long by the years, my desire
          not unlike a rock like this,
also crystal, porous, this weight,
not a rock you can depend on

      to keep its form, welcoming water,
         room for error, can I soften

the bolt. My jaw
    a buckle fastening tight: *sit*
        still, stay put, shut up—

The past a spiral staircase I climb,
bending over the railing to shout into the middle.

Letter to Another Immigrant Daughter

for Malvika

Were they dead honeybees or little beetles
you kept in a jar? A film canister. Isn't memory
impossible! I take copious photographs
against this inevitable outcome.
Failure, though, is essential to transformation.
You are citrus, hibiscus, what else?
At the park, her fingers in my hair, discussing
desire and theology, I'm reminded of our chats
about how to practice asking for what we really want.
Adnan wrote to Fawwaz, *I thus renounced the idea*
of writing you a formal letter on ' feminism',
and began living that which was given to me.
The backs of my knees are more sensitive than
I'd realized. I'm moved by the affection between
two men on the bus thundering about the difference
between the Dollar Tree and Dollar General—
I think good sex helps me adore the world.

There's What I Think and What I Feel

and I don't always know which is mine.
Cheek pressed against wood once alive.
When I see the cross on the hill

near Pilgrimage Bridge, part of me is kneeling
inside. I can't turn away fast enough.
Someone else's dreams were stitched

to this connective tissue before
I could give permission.
My nervous system

the closest thing to matrilineage.
Fragments linger in my philtrum,
little valley. *Zdrowaś Maryjo,*

łaski pełna. My weather app says
a nearby river is flooding.
Has shame ever saved anyone?

Voracious

I slip into bed, head full of tulips.
If devotion is measured
    in repetition, I'm inconsistent
      at best.

    Morning, Mary carved into a bar of soap in my fist,
ornamentation as protection, air of frankincense, voice of
      myrrh. Unsure about prayer, I waste confession
on a flickering screen,

      an island of plastic blooming
another floating downstream
      & up, likely stuck, too,
in my body's rivulets, yet I slice &
      seal a mango in another plastic baggy,
      remnants, cyclical
confession I am waist-high in
bruised fruit at the bottom
      of the sea bleached.

Midnight, face pressed again to a grip of tulips,
vivid-sweet, fresh, I want to swallow them whole.

Sometimes I pray
      before meals, more often forget, spitting out
    little bones from the same mouth I kiss my lover with.

Bodies of Hours

I left one of my bodies
in the Sangre de Cristo mountains

where the dunes rearranged before my eyes
through an invisible hourglass.

Eyelashes beating
against time.

Another charged up with dreams,
little batteries, that took me to the edge.

You have seen. The place with a view
and plunge. How wretched wanting can be.

Bits of glacier bluing
below sloping cliffs, dotting a vast sea.

I was in love then, stupid with it.
I saw the hue, but I didn't know. Blue is a memorial.

Color Keeps Time

or it rides us
like a torrent. Blurs
and fastens, flesh
to seconds. Just look
at your veins.
In vespertine woods,
I tried to read moss
by hand. There's
something laconic
about green that I need.

Lover, let the morning slow
time through the branches.

Magnolia

Blooming in stars, bells, cups, and saucers, before bees, before derelict cities.
I can't google you without involving the suspicious affliction of needing
to name, or the geopolitics of search engines. I just want your petals
casting shadows across my face. And to know if they are edible.
Many botanists say yes: raw, cooked, pickled, dried.
Must I consume to love?
Must I be consumed by love?
I trust you know the answer, pollinated by
beetles 95 million years ago. I pluck your sturdy petals, make
tea. Imagine I can read the desiccated pulp. A kind of sacrament
to taste and be tasted. When I am one day buried in the dirt, I offer my
frame, tissue, heart. You didn't ask me to live on like this. I'm asking you.

Letter to Another Immigrant Daughter

for Shilpi

Self splits from self.
Is it chaos, or the order of things?

Dancing in the desert,
when the barbed spine of a cholla cactus
attached itself to my right sneaker,
little dagger, alarmingly close,
burrowing into the heat of my pulse,
I thought, *We are trying*
to get close to the bone.

You know how. I want to live. Like an animal.

Reading Szymborska at Friday Harbor

Do I want more music from language?
Curled into myself against a floor-to-ceiling window,
I laugh about the Yeti poem, cry over her 1996 speech—
*Whatever inspiration is, it's born from a continuous
'I don't know.'* I read it in English.
In Polish school, I did not like her work.
I did not want to admit how much I don't know.
How many fields of oil burning. *The everlasting
snow*, melting. I'm watching an eagle
perched for the hunt, white-headed metronome.
Rapt, still I ask for song. Unspooling
in sound. How can I trust myself
when I am so seduced by beauty?
Scenic lookout, hot women on Instagram, denim
sky, muscle of petals. *I am not singing*,
says the eagle. A tired roar crowds my mouth.
When we drive down Sweet Pea Lane, Gabby says
so sweet it makes my teeth hurt. I write it down.

Letter to Another Immigrant Daughter

for Sarah

Days unclear, filled with sun. The flicker of another
  life coming for me. Rushing

makes an imprint—bruised knees. Time purpling
  the rhododendron. Near summer,

when childhood's shadow is near, you say you feel
  God's hand. Where on your back, exactly?

In my earliest memory, my father is teaching me
  how to make the sign of the cross

on the couch in a small apartment. Mama
  watches, a birthmark the shape of Polska

on her forearm. Meant for a better story.
  I wish for kinder eyes, to see less of everything.

Sometimes I go walking without my glasses.
  Maybe next time I'll spin in the grass,

arms wide open. I hope I'm laughing when I fall.
  I want to send that laughter to you.

A Kind of Weather

I may never move on ice in wordless
synchronicity like the skaters at dusk.

When one lowers her ear
to the frozen lake, they all kneel down. It is
to hear how coldness makes a surface of itself.

Where and when that surface might
rupture—fireflies in the chest.
Their cold bulbs
cracking.

.

To observe is the lesser
pleasure. Am I jealous of the skaters I invent?
Childhood's flicker in their possible chests.

What is called nostalgia is an attempt to track time.
At once forward and back, now circling.

Hunting the invented place, too,
for evidence.
Something hooved leaves desire lines.

.

Life is precious, monstrous, marked by tides.
I turn to the sea. Not for understanding.

.

Stretch my eyes beyond the instant.
My lover walks out the room.
Out the window a crow shits on the neighbor's roof.
Once I thought possessiveness was how to show love.
I press my finger to the space between my brows and push.

．

Saturated with image unshaped,
forming. A fern's shadow fine-tunes.
My attention chandeliers the present tense.
Not tense as fixture or decoration,
but a way to wear light. Like the heart
is worn, though people say not to.

I think the future wants something from me.

．

There are many lives I will never live.
Clouds of rain and smoke form
distantly. I get closer in my mind
to the Sangre de Cristo mountains.

If only to burn what I don't need.

．

I approach I approach I approach
but I take too long I take   I take
off my shoes   I put my feet
          where hooves left
imprints   in the dirt.

Dig a Cave into the Future

Hips against the counter. Lovers know.
Breath warms the kitchen but frost clings to the windows.

A woman sculpted in my mind. Her melting collarbone.
I ask for icicles. As in, suspension—no, preservation.

My longing a museum
I kneel into.

Sleet sounds like susurration when I'm dreaming
of the sea. Salt & swoon cupped close, every prayer

anchialine. No delirium like being
so thirsty.

What I want to see happen next
requires a protagonist with nerve.

A single narwhal joins a pod of belugas
1000km out of range. Some caves

are all bones & hunt,
some caves are imagined.

Cape Disappointment

Hundreds of years, and not a day passes
    that I'm not haunted.

Eternity. I swear it is her walking now
    through fog, wind, rain to reach me.

I recognize that coruscating gaze. She stops
    to see the milk the waves make. Once,

we watched them crash to dissolution
    on this very cliff. Their metallic lurch and

charge summoning the swoop of gulls. Lifting
    sand from the ocean floor to its longed-for gasp.

Behind her, I stepped closer. Pulled her hair
    back from her face. She said into my neck

before she left, [   ]. That was centuries ago.
    The woman I watch from this lighthouse is alone.

She has the face of someone who has lost everything
    except the central question of her life.

Memory hunts us both. She's walking toward me again.
    I can sense in her stride she will break open

each bolt fastening the entry. When she climbs
    the spiral stairs to where I've been waiting,

overlooking the Graveyard of the Pacific, wailing
　　winnowed by the ages, we will

scream and cry until even sound is made lonely.
　　When morning comes, I will comfort her.

She will be certain she comforts herself.

On Chronic Conditions

Fond of excess, I pour rosewater into rosebud tea. Drink it in a bath of rose salts.
Drop my pen in the water repeatedly.

Reading about how chronic stress rewires the brain, my fingers orbit the ever-present
knot in my neck. I can't remember when it first appeared.

•

Back flush against the physical therapist's table, I try to soften
the cave of my chest. In my efforts, I am kneaded and dragged.

Eventually, I am visited by flashes of sleep like bats.
The shock of wings fluttering me to an almost-gasp.
Their darkness so near but I don't make a sound.

•

I wake suddenly from a dream in which I'm en route to my hometown,
bile rising in my throat. Go to the kitchen for a glass of water,
wearing a garment that trails behind.

Someone following might trip over the train of silks and
cul-de-sacs, snakes, and lace. Bride to none
but rivers in pursuit of sea.

•

After trying acupuncture, little needle ghosts linger in my ears and feet.
I feel unbearably present. Permeable to the world.
I speed briefly down the hill to feel the slope of it.

•

Yelling does something strange to a child. It is a constant skittering.
Nervous system raked through over, and over, and over.

Well-meaning friends attempt to diagnose.

I'm on hold with the hospital. I'm on hold
with insurance. I'm on hold
with radiology. I'm on hold with
the gastroenterologist. I'm on hold
with otolaryngology. I'm on hold with billing. I'm on hold
and can't remember why.

I hope this   is temporary.
I fear I have inherited it.

I have inherited, for example, what my therapist calls a poverty mentality,
and more obviously ingrown toenails, a temper, fervor
for dreaming. Bunions, distrust, a need to be loved
to an obliterating degree. The immensity of their care.

•

Along the Chama River, Gregorian chants fill the chapel in lilt and echo.
I try not to fixate on the violence of the text.

Did I inherit a colonial mentality
from a people whose country was partitioned, disappeared
from the map? I come from a people who weren't colonizers,
but did they want to be?

All night it feels sinister. Stomach pain. Toenails purpling in the dim room.
Coyotes howling. Chest tight. Silence. In the aloneness I came for,
I claw at the sheets, praying *I cannot die yet.*

Morning's summer scene—swimsuit draped over the banister, tinkling chimes,
the baby goats' soft tongues—renders my sleeplessness embarrassing.

·

In the northwest, fingers firm around the oars, my friend's voice
is a low hum, saying, *this is not a land-or-sea place but a land-and-sea place.*

·

I chew my nails, scroll, retweet. Remember, vaguely, the relief of shooting the shit
as a teen, despite not getting the joke, not having seen the thing everyone
watched, learning to anticipate laughter, laughing along.

·

Near the shack once full of rats the feral barn cats were brought in to kill,
I watch the horses. Tails swishing. Sun dappling the deeply grooved back
of the horse abandoned for fifteen years, no food or shelter.
Now in good company.

·

I keep having to ask my beloveds to repeat themselves. Ears a hive, no honey.

My physical therapist cradles my head, turns it gently to a set of intolerable coordinates,
a land-and-sea place. But there's no sea, no boat, just nausea and a horizon

I'm turning away from. He asks questions in a calm tone. I'm breathing into
my belly. I'm staring at the ceiling trying not to puke.

.

Every baby on the plane is crying.

Heading to my childhood home, I shift shape,
try to find a comfortable seat. Reach for the names
of joints and muscles that increasingly hurt, names I knew back when I was dancing,
really dancing. Feeling for my foundation.

It wasn't just that I knew the names of body parts—I spoke to them.
I said things I can't explain.

On my teacup's brim, an idea about
womanness. Residue of the things I say
to appease. The things I don't say, do
they leave a mark? Sometimes family
functions as a form of surveillance.
It is felt thousands of miles away. I
associate arrows now with what comes
next, a kind of aim. I've had to relearn
laughter. Prayer coded first by a fixed,
locked box, and everything serious.
An ex once said I wasn't funny. I made
his friends laugh. Sometimes I fall in
love with potential, turn myself into a
bullseye. Scrolling tweets about WWIII.
The American thirst for spectacle. The
American urge to pretend we know
what the hell we are talking about.
One night on my first trip to Poland,
my cousin and I stayed up late making
up our own prayer. A momentary
sisterhood. Staring up at the ceiling
feeling the room unshape. Is a shape
always externally imposed? I can't
walk the distance between internal
and external. A man on the corner
holds a sign that reads: HELP IS ON
THE WAY TRUST GOD in red letters. I
think God has a sense of humor. I can
feel God laughing at me.

The Last Anchoress

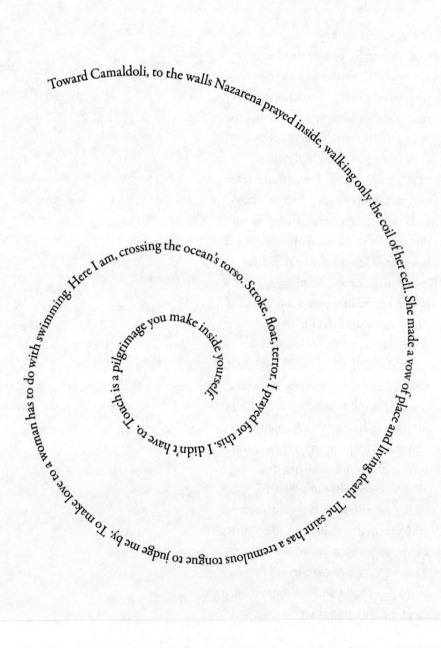

Toward Camaldoli, to the walls Nazarena prayed inside, walking only the coil of her cell. She made a vow of place and living death. The saint has a tremulous tongue to judge me by. To make love to a woman has to do with swimming. Here I am, crossing the ocean's torso. Stroke, float, terror. I prayed for this. I didn't have to. Touch is a pilgrimage you make inside yourself.

Kissing like There's No Place Else

You skated on and I became that fissure.
Walking on the lake, trying out a theory
of trust. I would carve your name

into limestone or quartzite if I carried anything
sharp or useful. Of course you have a pocketknife.
You have every tool you need.

I whistle across rock and plains as if I'm calling
to a dog. Some fantasies are pitifully domestic.
Enough firewood. Morning light across our wrists.

It's not dislocation I'm after but being moved
the way a picture was the very first time.
My first French kiss was at the movies. Kiss me!

like we are the history of cinema. Pull my hair,
cradle the head, call all the bees
to an impossibly wide field, unthought

in the pouring rain, where we're rolling now,
down the hill past the glow of meadows,
other loves, whole seasons,

the pulse the thaw the milk the sting,
no shore we can see, out to shipwreck.
Giving ourselves away. I would do it again.

Letter to Another Immigrant Daughter

for Sadia

We were brought here by stories we can't live
inside. The force with which the waterfall lets go
is full of angels. I want from faith the obliteration
of harm. How do I say it without violence? For
the preposition *of* to be a map without territory,
less a closed fist. I inherited devotion as a form.
Checklist in the language of law unto heaven.
Devotion stripped of intimacy has no song in it.
But we're singing.

To a Younger Self, Younger Than I Remember

You knew those hills to be a kind of curse,
and rolling down their viscous earth would signal

a descent into shadows, that vantage
from the edge of vision where

desire meets loss, where you prowl
despite yourself, wearing that dried leather

perfume made partly of castoreum, excavated
from nearby dams, the lily pads in your mouth

fresh and so still, for you're damming up entire rivers
in your blood (there's that whoosh and trickle

in your ears; must shadows be so loud?), orchestrating
the ground into the softest place you've ever landed, braiding

the grasses, which stretch and yawn green through the ages, but
you know no ages, only the singular age that you are

becoming, scent of pines
burning into

that heap of wood you carry then let splinter the roof
of your mouth, smoke on your tongue and

sorrow—even sirens blaring through town wouldn't
quiet your grief, let alone stop

you (I am reaching for
the part disappearing

behind the door facing the setting sun
in the hour between dog and wolf)

from washing your hair with pine tar
and dousing yourself in kerosene

before running toward the singed trees but
you didn't end up letting the wind take care of it

so, now that we're here together, time conducts
the vision exam—clearer? how about now?—to

make of us a long-lasting fragrance
emerging from the woods where

we do not have to burn
anything to taste fire

and that which doesn't seem to make a sound
is a sound inside resounding.

Worlds

We're boots in at low tide,
loosened. Generations cluster
into living sculptures.

The baby oyster attaches itself
to a remnant of another,
changes sex, reengineers the coastline.

No such thing as the world—I touch fragments.

I toss the top shell back into the sea
after hinge and sever.
No thought of pearls.

Salt and body are enough.
Fifty gallons of seawater
filtered in a day. I taste a fraction.

Anchor Baby

I keep close the intonation of my name
spoken in my mother's voice. There was a time
I let people mispronounce it. I don't

remember the sound of my grandfather's voice. I've lost
the word for the flower I could be, impatient
blossom, used to never wear lipstick, now I smear

shades of azalea on my lips, I kiss everything, I leave
a mark. Invocation. As in: a prayer I want
to repeat. The physicality of it: prayer, kissing, echoes

of a younger me. Trying to be approved of.
I'm not saying I am better now. I look up how to say
anchor in my first language. Once I didn't need

to search. Kotwica. My mama gave birth to me
a month after my parents arrived in the States.
Nie mówiła wtedy po angielsku. It was

her first time on a plane. I know nothing
of ground, of letting the ship sleep.
I fly for hours to visit. If I could

bind myself to a place, put cut flowers in a vase,
I would thank my mother that way. Instead
I pour the petals out.

On Belonging

Where do we go to find the myths that made us?

I can count on one hand the walks I've taken in the forest of my origin.
But a longing for return is built into the architecture of cities.

There is a rope
I'd like to follow
into a cave in myself.

•

Not quite chameleon, but
I long for every hue.
Slip on hooves, rearrange
scales, clip on wings.

A beloved texts, *There are entire worlds in you
you are denying.*

If I make of myself the mythical protagonist,
she must journey against fixed belonging.

•

In the office of dead letters,
unopened envelopes contain the other
writing. Addressed to the matrilineal.

Siphoning ink from the walls of a cave
that would engulf the Empire State,
if I could reach you. Rocks fall
in and out of love with time.

In one myth, Jacek went into the forest on the shortest day
for the flower that bloomed only on that longest night,
which he was told would secure his fortune. But he could not
share. And in his castle of aloneness he remained.

·

Searching for a feeling, I dig the wrong
way. Leaves beneath, tugging at the edges of my thinking
for a secret. Wilt is thick on the ground. I ache
to lie down. The wind intervenes, shifts my gaze: looking
could change me. But it isn't up to me.

Can't stop touching my hair. Flatten the curl.
Domesticate and dull. Comb and comb,
make it straight. A man who was never mine
gets a vasectomy. I may never give birth.

Lying on the floor in the dark, I light three candles.
I know there is a part of me that needs to die.
The radiators burn water from air.

Back to the veiled season
I once belonged to. Where all
the curtains hang just an inch off the floor.

What is the color of the inseam between the throat
and revelation? Revealed to grasses and no one else.

Carnations sleeping in teapots. Grief to pour out
for free, like it could water the acres.

Muscles along my neck knotted string I could tug
to a heap. Sweater undone sounds softer
than I mean. Little skeleton, unremembering.

I could take this grief on a walk.

.

I've walked where forest meets meadow, oxidized
iron turning the stream orange. Confronted with
my assumption of what is "natural."

I watch ashen butterflies on my friend's Instagram.
He tells me they are drinking water from the sand.
I picture Lake Michigan's shores. My parents returning
from work to a house whose gradients I know in the dark.

How many ecotones between us. Each one protecting
its neighbor. Some days distance protects me.

If I must make a quest of this, I will seek the freshwater
lake at the bottom of the sea.

Lately, I wake heavy stone unmoving, longing
for the feast of current which sees the shape of the earth.
So I log on to Twitter thirsty. Watch language rushing past.

Do we choose the questions
our lives ask?

.

A hundred questions I want to ask
my great-grandmother, whose face I can only
imagine. From what scraps I've gathered from
her untold life, she belonged most to God.

Prayer with no covenant but fervor,
incense, bronze; the desire for excess
I inherited, doctrine of beauty in excess,

tub full of lilacs, smearing jasmine on my neck,
careful pressure on the cervical flexors, which
bind the base of the skull to the image

that erects and rotates the spine,
where bitterness toward mothers lives.
How she wasted hours devoted

to someone neglecting said hours, chasing instead
distraction, and some days I am like him, damn it,
made bitter in my nearness, and tending to

that image. Family constructs in us
the sacred and profane. Forming a covenant.

If belonging is form,
its constraints erode the land.
Recurring floods.

•

Enlarging the pixels of faces I adore to make
of desire more than crude representation,
I note each instrument in this orchestra.

Undressed by music, root:
muse. Even when there doesn't seem to be
a sound, there is something being plucked
inside. Muse is a state with no governing body.

I want body, I want form.
Without the rot of control. I grip
the edges of roses decaying almost to paper,
weighing petal's etchings
against the highways of my blood.

Must I compare. Petal I
tore off scrutinized in laptop light. Awake
thinking of upside-down roses my mother
hung to dry. Cerise, flushed, fading.
On the coast, I missed Chicago winter.

Meaning I'd forgotten
what it's like.

Discomfort is a sacred site.
Listen closer for the night beyond
engines. Ants parading down a leaf.

If I could get that quiet.
If silence grew unwounding. As if.

As if a body is a field and the field
is a carnival against loss.
Here there is no Ferris wheel.
I can't compare loss to anything.

Can you belong to what you've lost?

•

I bring the river questions.
Ghosts sit with backs turned to its bank.
River speaks in reverse elegy.

I sense the turning of keys, mystery
and resistance to mystery, the empty
sensation I mistake for hunger—Winter
in me, cavernous, and caves beyond

the one whose entrance I pace, a beckoning
that terrifies and thrills, an inwardness that haunts
the pelvic floor, a flickering there,
restless, fluttering at the faintest

stressor—a thought—as indicated by the machine
I'm hooked up to in the pelvic PT's nondescript office,
watching little spikes advance across the screen.
Overengaged, the muscles are tired and weak.

Working so hard, yet it is difficult to even locate
my pelvic floor with my mind. It seems
to be doing the work of my unconscious.
What else is working in me?

The cave is filled with kelp and anemones
clutching slivers of glass—so sparkly—
like a feast.   (If/when

    glass enters the bloodstream try not to panic
        you can cry you can drink detox tea phone a friend
    take the call in the tub go to urgent care

        it is generally not recommended you rage re: current systems of
    care/lack thereof if you must you might rage against
        the sharp edges) those little glittering mirrors
refracting light.

                                    •

This could be a story of perpetual
shedding. Is it tragic to want
to explain myself?

Taught to fear snakes, I've lost time.
There's a ticking clock on self-deceit.

My family has an idea about belonging like a flag
that stretches and shrinks in the wind.

Is a nation more or less than a shared language?
My grandfather was born near a city I call by its Polish
name, belonging now to another nation.

Carry me, beyond the symbol, to the vivid thing—
Please, God. Surprise a symbol into music.

No surprise my hips are tight and rain is coming
down. I know about epigenetic memory,
bad things stored in tight spots.
But what joys?

Some joy passed down to me
is a kind of performance—
my mother could have been a star.

Instead of mapping apocalypse onto
this place, I'll make a shadowgraph.

See how shadow shapes the land. In drought,
the bees tune pollination to an A note.

Wished-for bell. Vibrating the anther.
In hushed tones. Near-rain, the smell.

Once-meadow cracking.
From air's vantage, it's dust

and nothing but.
Thirst makes record.

.

Cixous writes, *my desires have invented
new desires*—yes, I speak to you
in sweat. Against the implied condition
of property assigned to me. I'm searching
for belonging beyond possession,
a depth of care. Some days I care
in theory, touched only
by the image, denying
my relationship to the hours.

Do I belong to the hours?

Questions huddle
before the hunt.

.

I'm rolling around on the floor again,
breathing into my extremities.
Practice keeping the vital center intact.

This reaching is for nowhere I am
trying to arrive.

Like skipping stones to build underwater
a doorless vault of feeling.

Do we belong to ghosts
or do ghosts belong to us?

If, standing, I tilt the bowl of my pelvis
forward, slightly, soft bend in the knees,
run my tongue across my teeth, and steadily
lift my arms—slower—wrists and fingers slack—
hands that gesture through curve toward holding but,
facing the ground instead, are letting go—and reach
back, just enough to make a soft arch of my back,
I can sometimes feel the many arches,
all that bone and music, twisted up inside. I imagine
gateway after gateway I have kept from myself.

•

For years I lived like a piano hiding its strings.
Doesn't something in us refuse
to be tuned?

Once I loved to play legato, holding
the pedal a beat too long when
the notes were supposed to detach.

Yes, there are songs without flags.

I dream I see a river rise like a tide.
Swiftly, under the bridge it rises
to form an arch, separating the water
from its bed, and out walk the people
of the river, onto the banks, the river's dead.

If spirits take up a home in us, may they rest
where we touch dirt, where breath goes,
where a strong grip strains for music.

·

Beneath the day's sensuous material an under-
growth. Imagine peeling the bitter rind of every myth
and smelling like citrus after hours. I swear I'll stop talking
about the hours we cannot own.

I am looking for the place
where the trees unmake our image.

I came to dig and I can't say
who asked me to kiss the ground
and wipe away the evidence.

Bury the Anchor

How will you begin? —BHANU KAPIL

Left foot into the stirrup, swing my right leg over
Larkspur, jonquil, rhododendron
Sing the second song that comes to mind; slip the first into memory's crater
Beeswax, a pocketknife, kettle on low
Demand the fog tell how
Feel myself a stone at the bottom of a well
No, the sea
Rinse
It has to do with extremities
Throw open the curtains the way my mother did, perhaps her mother &
    mother before
Bury the anchor
Go to the lake
Arrange the fragments
Shaping—dreaming—

Beloved,

you gather me. I am not petals, though I have eaten wildflowers on greens in that glow particular to the other planet, as Miłosz described it, that is California, where I walked through salt and fog and found Mary enshrined in chalk on a gash of rock and watched the waves devour themselves til my phone died, so that I was forced to rely on the generosity of strangers, and I did take a photo later of said plate, marveling while sending it to you from the aloneness I'd traveled there to make something out of. Please send a photo of your face. Is it not my purpose to see where, exactly, laughter has rivered around the eyes I adore? There was a donkey in Petaluma with a soft, steady gaze. I will not turn away from the ache of this world. I'm trying to feel my feet. Let's cry enough to submerge, up to our ankles at least. Don't keep your grief from me.

Notes

The epigraph from Wisława Szymborska appears in her collected *Wiersze wszystkie* (Znak, 2023).

"Failed Essay on Repressed Sexuality": The title is indebted to Elisa Gonzalez's "Failed Essay on Privilege," from her book *Grand Tour*.

"Salt of the Earth": The italicized text is from articles using the phrase *anchor baby* in *Forbes*, *The Los Angeles Times*, NPR.org, and *Oxford English Dictionary*.

"On Self-Deceit": The full title of the Francesca Woodman photograph referenced is *Self-Deceit #1 (Roma)*.

"Letter to Another Immigrant Daughter": This series grew out of an epistolary exchange with the poet Sarah Ghazal Ali. The poem for Joyce Chen adapts a line from an interview with Björk and Ocean Vuong from *AnOther Magazine*, in which Björk says, "When warming up your voice, it's almost like you're building a cathedral inside your skull."

"Archival": I was invited to create a workshop in conversation with sculptor Diana Al-Hadid's "Archive of Longings" exhibit at the Henry Art Gallery in 2021. This work engaged historical, mythological, and biblical narratives of women, as well as questions of migration and collective history. Al-Hadid wrote, in the label for one of her sculptures, "I wondered how much of myself I could lose and still be there." I remain riveted by the question.

"Borderwound": The Gloria Anzaldúa quote comes from her book *Borderlands/La Frontera: The New Mestiza*.

"Holding Ground": The italicized text is from the Wikipedia entry "anchor."

"Because Horse Is the Closest I Can Get to It": This title is the second line in Jack Gilbert's poem "Finding Something," in *The Great Fires*.

"Wilno": The italicized text is from Adam Mickiewicz's epic poem, *Pan Tadeusz*. The literal translation of the Polish word *ojczyzna* is "fatherland."

"Letter to Another Immigrant Daughter": The italicized text in the "Letter to Another Immigrant Daughter" for Malvika is from Etel Adnan's *Of Cities & Women (Letters to Fawwaz)*.

"Magnolia": The name of a poetic form, "The Cradle-Magnolia," came to me in a dream, and I ignored the invitation to write into it for a couple years, before finally writing "Magnolia." The form's constraints include: a poem of twelve lines that steadily shorten to cradle two questions in the middle, before lengthening back out; a direct address to a natural element/living thing; a reference or engagement with something revealed in a dream. Let me know if you write one.

"Reading Szymborska at Friday Harbor": This poem is indebted to Aria Aber's "Reading Rilke at Lake Mendota, Wisconsin." The italicized text is from Wisława Szymborska's acceptance speech for the 1996 Nobel Prize in Literature and from her poem "Notes from a Nonexistent Himalayan Expedition," translated by Stanisław Barańczak and Clare Cavanagh.

"Dig a Cave into the Future": The title is adapted from a line in *W Magazine*, in which Björk interviews herself: "you have to imagine something that doesn't exist and dig a cave into the future and demand space."

"Worlds": This poem borrows from a line I came across while reading Jenny Offill's *Dept. of Speculation*, attributed to Keats: "No such thing as the world becoming an easy place to save your soul in." I kept thinking about the first part, "No such thing as the world," an idea which troubles and allures me. A couple years after writing the poem, I encountered this passage in Hélène Cixous' *Three Steps on the Ladder of Writing*, translated by Sarah Cornell and Susan Sellers, which has opened up this poem for me: "...to be human we need to experience the end of the world. We need to lose the world, to lose a world, and to discover that there is more than one world..."

"On Belonging": The Hélène Cixous quote is from her essay "The Laugh of the Medusa," translated by Keith Cohen and Paula Cohen in 1976. My thinking on belonging is also indebted to Dionne Brand's *A Map to the Door of No Return: Notes to Belonging*.

"Bury the Anchor": This poem is indebted to Bhanu Kapil's *The Vertical Interrogation of Strangers*—I wrote it in response to the third of her twelve questions: "How will you begin?"

Acknowledgements

Thank you to the editors of the following publications where earlier versions of these poems first appeared: *128 Lit*, *Columbia Journal*, *Hypertext Magazine*, *Shenandoah*, *Hobart*, *Hayden's Ferry Review*, *BOAAT*, *Michigan Quarterly Review*, *Palette Poetry*, *Waxwing*, *Ninth Letter*, *Redivider*, *The Maine Review*, *Bellingham Review*, *Poetry Northwest*, *Passages North*, *Sporklet*, *Sundog Lit*, *Southeast Review*, *TriQuarterly*, *The Adroit Journal*, *SAND Journal*, *Gulf Coast*, *West Branch*, *The Los Angeles Review*, *SWWIM*, *Moss*, *The Atlantic*, as well as *Poetry Daily*, *The Slowdown* podcast, *Escape Tunnels* from Small Craft Advisory Press, and the *Here to Stay: Poetry and Prose from the Undocumented Diaspora* anthology.

This book emerged thanks to childhood dreams, my parents' sacrifices, deep study and voracious reading beyond institutions, conversations across art forms, poets living and long gone, rivers & lakes & the sea. It takes many co-conspirators to bring a book into the world—the following is only a partial list.

Thank you to my editor, Alyssa Ogi, for your brilliance and precision, and the entire team at Tin House for your care. Justin Rigamonti and the Carolyn Moore Writing Residency for your belief in this project. Macy Chadwick and In Cahoots Residency for the grant that brought me to Petaluma's storybook hills. The Whiteley Center for big windows, time reading Szymborska, a visit from a black fox. Abbey Freed Holden for the casita daydream. Dodge Poetry Festival for the honor of being in conversation with luminaries. Brooklyn Poets for the fellowship and gift of working with Xan Phillips. The Jack Straw

Fellowship and E.J. Koh. The singular Shira Erlichman and In Surreal Life. The AWP Writer to Writer program and Jehanne Dubrow as I returned to poems, full of doubt. To poetry bookstores, Innisfree (thank you, Brian Buckley) and Open Books: A Poem Emporium (thank you, Billie Swift).

Gabrielle Bates, you changed my life! Thank you, Erin Marie Lynch, Erin McCoy, and Gabby, for our writing group where I honed the magic of revision, encountered rigor matched by no classroom. Sarah Ghazal Ali, may we write letters in poems as long as we live. For a depth of care I'm in bad debt to, that "place of refuge" Moten & Harney speak of: Shilpi Gupta, Isaac Javier Rivera, Kyle Huelsman, Colin Delargy, Ali Bibbo, Marjorie Davidson.

For vital conversations, insight, and support: Aria Aber, Malvika Jolly, Britt McGillivray, Quenton Baker, Elisa Gonzalez, Sadia Hassan, Joyce Chen, I.S. Jones, Bretty Rawson, Tiana Clark, Cy X, David Naimon, Lucie Bonvalet, Luther Hughes, Jeric Smith, Steven Espada Dawson, Vanessa Angélica Villarreal, Miriam Milena, Arisa White, Taneum Bambrick, Lauren Samblanet, Nanya Jhingran, Rachel Edelman, Laura Da', Abbie Kiefer, Shara McCallum, Anastacia-Reneé, Nora Alwah. For their generous readings and support of this collection: Victoria Chang, Camonghne Felix, Joanna Klink.

I started my MFA at UW-Madison as I was putting the finishing touches on this book, where I wrote its crucial final poems. Thank you to Paula Tran, Amy Quan Barry, Erika Meitner, and to the finest cohort to ever do it: Maryhilda Obasiota Ibe, Iqra Khan, juj lepe, Jonny Teklit, Andrew Chi Keong Yim. To Chessy Normile, Mandy Moe Pwint Tu, Andrew & our incarcerated students at Oak Hill. To the UW-Madison Graduate School for funding that helped me return to Poland after a decade—I reviewed proofs of these pages on a train bound for the Bałtyk sea, landscapes flickering out the window.

Thank you to my parents, Danuta and Leszek Humienik, for your immeasurable courage, sacrifice, and care. Kocham Was. Your dreams had dreams. Dziękuję.

NICHOLAS NICHOLS

PATRYCJA HUMIENIK, daughter of Polish immigrants, is a writer, editor, and performance artist. She has developed writing and movement workshops for the Henry Art Gallery, Arts + Literature Laboratory, Northwest Film Forum, in prisons, and elsewhere. An MFA candidate at UW-Madison, she serves as the events director for The Seventh Wave, where she is also an editor for the Community Anthologies project. Patrycja grew up in Evanston, Illinois, and lives in Madison, Wisconsin.